• Cooking for Today •

THAI COOKING

· *Cooking for Today* ·

THAI COOKING

CAROL BOWEN

Produced by Kingfisher Design, London
for
Parragon
13 Whiteladies Road
Clifton
Bristol BS8 1PB

ISBN 0-75252-878-5

Printed in Italy

Reprinted in 1998

Acknowledgements:

Design & DTP: Pedro & Frances Prá-Lopez / Kingfisher Design
Art Direction: Clive Hayball
Managing Editor: Alexa Stace
Special Photography: Martin Brigdale
Home Economist: Jill Eggleton
Step-by-Step Photography: Karl Adamson
Step-by-Step Home Economist: Joanna Craig
Stylist: Helen Trent

Food kindly supplied by B E International Foods Ltd

Photographs on pages 6, 18, 28, 52 & 64: reproduced by permission of
ZEFA Picture Library (UK) Ltd

Note:

Cup measurements in this book are for American cups. Tablespoons are assumed to be 15 ml.
Unless otherwise stated, milk is assumed to be full-fat, eggs are standard size 2
and pepper is freshly ground black pepper.

Contents

CHAPTER ONE

Starters

From the spicy exuberance of a hot and sour duck salad to the more subtle flavours of a chicken or beef satay, the importance of the starter-style dish has long been recognised and celebrated in Thai households. Unlike Western cuisine, however, it is more likely to be served before a meal with drinks, as a snack between meals, as party or celebration food, or as a dish that is served just before and then with the main course.

Typically several dishes of this type are served at once in the age-old tradition of enticing and tempting the appetite or teasing the palate. In the pages that follow you will find a selection of such tempting entrées from baby fish cakes with a tasty cucumber garnish; tiny skewered chicken or beef kebabs called satay that are served with a flavoursome peanut sauce; a colourful array of crisp vegetable crudités served with a Thai shrimp dipping sauce; and mouth-watering hot and sour or sweet and sour crisp salad mixtures.

Fortunately for the cook these are dishes that can be prepared well ahead of time or can be assembled and cooked very quickly. Consider too some of the main-course recipes in bite-sized portions – Bangkok Barbecued Chicken Legs and Duckling with Ginger and Lime Dressing double up beautifully as starter or main course fare.

Opposite: *The fishing fleet returns at sunset to Kata Beach, Phuket.*

STEP 2

RED CURRY FISHCAKES

*Just the thing to entice the tastebuds, Thai fishcakes make a tasty starter
and good introduction to a Thai-style meal. Almost
any kind of fish fillets or seafood can be used.*

MAKES ABOUT 24 (TO SERVE 4-6)

*1 kg/2 lb fish fillets or prepared seafood,
    such as cod, haddock, prawns (shrimp),
    crab meat or lobster
1 egg, beaten
2 tbsp chopped fresh coriander
Red Curry Paste (see page 30)
1 bunch spring onions (scallions), finely
    chopped
vegetable oil, for deep-frying
chilli flowers, to garnish*

CUCUMBER SALAD:
*1 large cucumber, peeled and grated
2 shallots, peeled and grated
2 red chillies, seeded and very finely chopped
2 tbsp fish sauce
2 tbsp dried powdered shrimps
1$\frac{1}{2}$-2 tbsp lime juice*

1 Place the fish in a blender or food
processor with the egg, coriander
and curry paste and purée until smooth
and well blended.

2 Turn the mixture into a bowl, add
the spring onions (scallions) and
mix well to combine.

3 Taking 2 tablespoons of the fish
mixture at a time, shape into balls,

STEP 3

then flatten them slightly with your
fingers to make fishcakes.

4 Heat the oil in a wok or pan until
hot, add a few of the fishcakes and
deep-fry for a few minutes until brown
and cooked through. Remove with a
slotted spoon and drain on paper towels.
Keep warm while cooking the remaining
fishcakes.

5 Meanwhile, to make the cucumber
salad, mix the cucumber with the
shallots, chillies, fish sauce, dried shrimps
and lime juice.

6 Serve the salad immediately, with
the warm fishcakes.

STEP 4

CHILLIES

When handling chillies be very careful not
to touch your face or eyes: chilli juice is a
powerful irritant, and can be very painful
on the skin. Always wash your hands after
preparing chillies.

STEP 5

CRUDITES WITH SHRIMP SAUCE

This is a classic Thai starter – fruit and vegetable crudités served with a spicy, garlicky shrimp sauce. It is served at every meal, and each family has their own favourite recipe.

STEP 1

SERVES 6

about 750 g/1½ lb prepared raw fruit and vegetables, such as broccoli, cauliflower, apple, pineapple, cucumber, celery, (bell) peppers and mushrooms

SAUCE:
60 g/2 oz dried shrimps
1 cm/½ in cube shrimp paste
3 garlic cloves, crushed
4 red chillies, seeded and chopped
6 stems fresh coriander, coarsely chopped
juice of 2 limes
fish sauce, to taste
brown sugar, to taste

1 Soak the dried shrimps in warm water for 10 minutes.

2 To make the sauce, place the shrimp paste, drained shrimps, garlic, chillies and coriander in a food processor or blender and process until well chopped but not smooth.

3 Turn the sauce mixture into a bowl and add the lime juice, mixing well.

4 Add fish sauce and brown sugar to taste to the sauce, mixing to blend well. Cover the bowl tightly and chill the sauce in the refrigerator for at least 12 hours, or overnight.

5 To serve, arrange the fruit and vegetables attractively on a large serving plate. Place the prepared sauce in the centre for dipping.

STEP 2

STEP 3

STEP 4

ALTERNATIVE

Hard-boiled quail's eggs are often added to this traditional fruit and vegetable platter and certainly would be offered on a special occasion.

STEP 2

STEP 3

STEP 4

STEP 5

SWEET & SOUR TOFU SALAD

Tofu (bean curd) is a delicious, healthy alternative to meat. Mixed with a variety of crisp stir-fried vegetables, then tossed in a piquant sweet and sour dressing, it makes an ideal light meal or starter.

SERVES 4-6

2 tbsp vegetable oil
1 garlic clove, crushed
500 g/1 lb tofu (bean curd), cubed
1 onion, sliced
1 carrot, cut into julienne strips
1 stick celery, sliced
2 small red (bell) peppers, cored, seeded and
  sliced
250 g/8 oz mangetout (snow peas),
  trimmed and halved
125 g/4 oz broccoli, trimmed and divided
  into florets
125g/4 oz thin green beans, halved
2 tbsp oyster sauce
1 tbsp tamarind concentrate
1 tbsp fish sauce
1 tbsp tomato purée (paste)
1 tbsp light soy sauce
1 tbsp chilli sauce
2 tbsp sugar
1 tbsp white vinegar
pinch of ground star anise
1 tsp cornflour (cornstarch)
300 ml/¹/₂ pint/1¹/₄ cups water

1 Heat the vegetable oil in a large, heavy-based frying pan or wok until hot. Add the crushed garlic and cook for a few seconds.

2 Add the tofu in batches and stir-fry over a gentle heat, until golden on all sides. Remove with a slotted spoon and keep warm.

3 Add the onion, carrot, celery, red (bell) pepper, mangetout (snow peas), broccoli and green beans to the pan and stir-fry for about 2-3 minutes or until tender-crisp.

4 Add the oyster sauce, tamarind concentrate, fish sauce, tomato purée (paste), soy sauce, chilli sauce, sugar, vinegar and star anise, mixing well to blend. Stir-fry for a further 2 minutes.

5 Mix the cornflour (cornstarch) with the water and add to the pan with the fried tofu. Stir-fry gently until the sauce boils and thickens slightly.

6 Serve the salad immediately, on warm plates.

STEP 1

STEP 2

STEP 3

STEP 5

CHICKEN OR BEEF SATAY

A favourite Thai dish that can be made with chicken or beef and served with a spicy peanut sauce.

SERVES 4-6

4 boneless, skinned chicken breasts or
    750 g/1½ lb rump steak, trimmed

MARINADE:
1 small onion, finely chopped
1 garlic clove, crushed
2.5 cm/1 in piece ginger root, peeled and
    grated
2 tbsp dark soy sauce
2 tsp chilli powder
1 tsp ground coriander
2 tsp dark brown sugar
1 tbsp lemon or lime juice
1 tbsp vegetable oil

SAUCE:
300 ml/½ pint/1¼ cups coconut milk
4 tbsp/⅓ cup crunchy peanut butter
1 tbsp fish sauce
1 tsp lemon or lime juice
salt and pepper

1 Trim any fat from the chicken or beef then cut into thin strips, about 7 cm/3 in long.

2 To make the marinade, place all the ingredients in a shallow dish and mix well. Add the chicken or beef strips and turn in the marinade until well coated. Cover and leave to marinate for 2 hours or stand overnight in the refrigerator.

3 Remove the meat from the marinade and thread the pieces, concertina style, on bamboo or thin wooden skewers.

4 Grill the chicken and beef satays for 8-10 minutes, turning and brushing occasionally with the marinade, until cooked through.

5 Meanwhile, to make the sauce, mix the coconut milk with the peanut butter, fish sauce and lemon juice in a pan. Bring to the boil and cook for 3 minutes. Season to taste and serve with the cooked satays.

SATAY STICKS

Fine bamboo or wooden skewers are traditionally used to cook satays. Soak in cold water for at least one hour to prevent them from burning and scorching during cooking.

HOT AND SOUR DUCK SALAD

This is a lovely tangy salad, drizzled with a lime juice and Thai fish sauce dressing. It makes a splendid starter or light main course dish.

STEP 1

Serves 4

2 heads crisp salad lettuce, washed and
    separated into leaves
2 shallots, thinly sliced
4 spring onions (scallions), chopped
1 celery stick, finely sliced into julienne
    strips
5 cm/2 in piece cucumber, cut into julienne
    strips
125 g/4 oz bean-sprouts
1 x 200 g/7 oz can water chestnuts, drained
    and sliced
4 duck breast fillets, roasted and sliced (see
    page 43)
orange slices, to serve

Dressing:
3 tbsp fish sauce
1 1/2 tbsp lime juice
2 garlic cloves, crushed
1 red chilli pepper, seeded and very finely
    chopped
1 green chilli pepper, seeded and very finely
    chopped
1 tsp palm or demerara sugar

1 Mix the lettuce leaves with the shallots, spring onions (scallions), celery, cucumber, bean-sprouts and water chestnuts. Place the mixture on a large serving platter.

2 Arrange the duck breast slices on top of the salad in an attractive overlapping pattern.

3 To make the dressing, put the fish sauce, lime juice, garlic, chillies and sugar into a small pan. Heat gently, stirring constantly. Taste and adjust the piquancy if liked by adding more lime juice, or add more fish sauce to reduce the sharpness.

4 Drizzle the warm salad dressing over the duck salad and serve immediately.

STEP 2

STEP 3

JULIENNE STRIPS

To cut vegetables into julienne strips, first slice thinly into even-sized slices. Stack the slices on top of each other, then cut with a sharp knife into very thin shreds.

STEP 4

CHAPTER TWO

Fish & Shellfish

It is not surprising that fish and shellfish feature prominently on the typical Thai menu, so much of the country is surrounded by water. Whole fresh fish are often simply charcoal-grilled, steamed, fried or baked. Many are baked in banana leaves to keep the flesh moist and succulent. Seafood is often skewered and barbecued or sizzled in a wok with rice, chillies, nuts and other finely sliced or diced vegetables to make a quick and tasty one-pot meal. Both fish and seafood are also given the pungent-flavoured treatment in a whole host of curries from mild and mellow to fiery and fierce. Fruit such as pineapple, papaya and mango may also be added to give a flavour and texture contrast.

Whatever the fish the golden rule is to choose seafood that is absolutely at the peak of freshness. Look for whole fish that has bright eyes, red gills, firm flesh, shiny scales and a fresh sea-like odour. Never settle for second best! Likewise choose shellfish that is still tightly locked and closed in its shell. Discard those that are already open.

Opposite: *Fishing boats moored on Chon Khram beach, Koh Samui Island. The seas around Thailand teem with fish of every kind.*

STEP 1

STEP 2

STEP 3

STEP 4

FRIED RICE & PRAWNS (SHRIMP)

When you've got one eye on the clock and a meal to make this is the one!
Made in a trice, yet simply stunning to look at,
its taste belies its simplicity.

SERVES 4

60 g/ 2 oz/ ¼ cup butter
3 tbsp vegetable oil
500 g/ 1 lb/ 3 cups cooked basmati rice
6 spring onions (scallions), finely sliced
125 g/4 oz mangetout (snow peas), halved
1 carrot, cut into fine julienne strips
125 g/4 oz canned water chestnuts, drained
  and sliced
1 small crisp lettuce, shredded
350 g/ 12 oz peeled tiger prawns (shrimp)
1 large red chilli, seeded and sliced
  diagonally
3 egg yolks
4 tsp sesame oil
salt and pepper

1 Heat the butter and the oil in a large, heavy-based frying pan or wok. Add the cooked rice and stir-fry for 2 minutes.

2 Add the spring onions (scallions), mangetout (snow peas), carrot, water chestnuts and salt and pepper to taste, mixing well. Stir-fry over medium heat for a further 2 minutes.

3 Add the shredded lettuce, prawns (shrimp) and chilli and stir-fry for a further 2 minutes.

4 Beat the egg yolks with the sesame oil and stir into the pan, coating the rice and vegetable mixture. Cook for about 2 minutes to set the egg mixture.

5 Serve the rice and prawns (shrimp) at once on warmed plates.

FRIED RICE

For perfect fried rice, it is best to cook the rice ahead of time and allow it to cool completely before adding to the hot oil. In that way the rice grains will remain separate, and the rice will not become lumpy or heavy.

SIZZLED CHILLI PRAWNS (SHRIMP)

Another Thai classic – large prawns (shrimp) marinated in a chilli mixture then stir-fried with cashews. Serve with a fluffy rice and braised vegetables.

STEP 1

SERVES 4

5 tbsp soy sauce
5 tbsp dry sherry
3 dried red chillies, seeded and chopped
2 garlic cloves, crushed
2 tsp grated ginger root
5 tbsp water
625 g/ 1¼ lb shelled tiger prawns (shrimp)
1 large bunch spring onions (scallions), chopped
90 g/ 3 oz/⅔ cup salted cashew nuts
3 tbsp vegetable oil
2 tsp cornflour (cornstarch)

1 Mix the soy sauce with the sherry, chillies, garlic, ginger and water in a large bowl.

2 Add the prawns (shrimp), spring onions (scallions) and cashews and mix well. Cover tightly and leave to marinate for at least 2 hours, stirring occasionally.

3 Heat the oil in a large, heavy-based frying pan or wok. Drain the prawns (shrimp), spring onions (scallions) and cashews from the marinade with a slotted spoon and add to the pan, reserving the marinade. Stir-fry over a high heat for 1-2 minutes.

4 Mix the reserved marinade with the cornflour (cornstarch), add to the pan and stir-fry for about 30 seconds, until the marinade forms a slightly thickened shiny glaze over the prawn (shrimp) mixture.

5 Serve the prawns (shrimp) immediately, with rice.

STEP 2

VARIATION

For an attractive presentation serve this dish on mixed wild rice and basmati or other long-grain rice. Start cooking the wild rice in boiling water. After 10 minutes, add the basmati rice or other rice and continue boiling until all grains are tender. Drain well and adjust the seasoning.

STEP 3

STEP 4

PINEAPPLE & FISH CURRY

This is a fiery hot Thai curry dish all the better for serving with refreshing (and cooling) fresh pineapple pieces.

STEP 1

STEP 2a

STEP 2b

STEP 3

SERVES 4

2 pineapples
7 cm/ 3 in piece galangal, sliced
2 blades of lemon grass, bruised then chopped
5 sprigs fresh basil
500 g/ 1 lb firm white fish fillets, cubed (monkfish, halibut or cod, for example)
125 g/4 oz peeled prawns (shrimp)
2 tbsp vegetable oil
2 tbsp Red Curry Paste (see page 30)
125 ml/4 fl oz/¹/₂ cup thick coconut milk or cream
2 tbsp fish sauce
2 tsp palm or demarara sugar
2-3 red chillies, seeded and cut into thin julienne strips
about 6 kaffir lime leaves, torn into pieces
coriander sprigs, to garnish

1 Cut the pineapples in half lengthways. Remove the flesh, reserving the shells if using (see right). Remove the core from the pineapple flesh then dice into bite-sized pieces.

2 Place the galangal in a large shallow pan with the lemon grass and basil. Add the fish cubes and just enough water to cover. Bring to the boil, reduce the heat and simmer for about 2 minutes. Add the prawns (shrimp) and cook for a further 1 minute or until the fish is just cooked. Remove from the flavoured stock with a slotted spoon and keep warm.

3 Heat the oil in a heavy-based pan or wok. Add the curry paste and cook for 1 minute. Stir in the coconut milk or cream, fish sauce, brown sugar, chillies and lime leaves.

4 Add the pineapple and cook until just heated through. Add the cooked fish and mix gently to combine.

5 Spoon into the reserved pineapple shells, if liked, and serve immediately, garnished with sprigs of coriander.

VARIATION

This dish could be served on plates, but for a stunning presentation on a special occasion, serve in the hollowed-out shells of the pineapple.

WRAPPED FISH WITH GINGER

This is fish cooked in a healthy, palate-tingling way. Whole mackerel or trout are stuffed with herbs, wrapped in foil or, more authentically, banana leaves, baked and then drizzled with a fresh ginger butter.

STEP 1

STEP 2a

STEP 2b

STEP 3

SERVES 4

OVEN: 190°C/375°F/GAS 5

4 x 250 g/8 oz whole trout or mackerel,
    gutted
4 tbsp chopped fresh coriander
5 garlic cloves, crushed
2 tsp grated lemon or lime zest
2 tsp vegetable oil
banana leaves, for wrapping (optional)
90 g/3 oz/6 tbsp butter
1 tbsp grated ginger root
1 tbsp light soy sauce
salt and pepper
coriander sprigs and lemon or lime wedges,
    to garnish

1 Wash and dry the fish. Mix the coriander with the garlic, lemon or lime zest and salt and pepper to taste. Spoon into the fish cavities.

2 Brush the fish with a little oil, season well and place each fish on a double thickness sheet of baking parchment or foil and wrap up well to enclose. Alternatively, wrap in banana leaves (see right).

3 Place on a baking tray and bake in the preheated oven for about 25 minutes or until the flesh will flake easily.

4 Meanwhile, melt the butter in a small pan. Add the grated ginger and stir until well mixed, then stir in the soy sauce.

5 To serve, unwrap the fish parcels, drizzle over the ginger butter and garnish with coriander and lemon or lime wedges.

BANANA LEAVES

For a really authentic touch, wrap the fish in banana leaves, which can be ordered from specialist oriental supermarkets. They are not edible, but impart a delicate flavour to the fish.

27

CHAPTER THREE

Meat & Poultry

Unlike many other Oriental nationalities, the Thais are not restricted by religion over what they can eat, so pork, beef and lamb appear with poultry on the menu. However, since quantities can be scarce by Western standards, the Thais invent imaginative dishes that cunningly stretch limited supplies to the full.

Hence you will find wonderful meats stretched with noodles, chicken stir-fried with an array of vegetables, beef extended with glistening shredded bok choy cabbage, and meats simmered and stretched with vegetables in a coconut milk and chilli paste sauce.

You'll also find some old favourites with the Thai inspirational twist – chicken roasted with the addition of lemon grass, kaffir lime leaves, ginger, coriander and garlic; and fried beef steak, the steak cut into strips and stir-fried with coloured (bell) peppers, spring onions (scallions), celery, mushrooms, onions and crunchy cashew nuts, all the better for serving with a mound of fluffy rice and a few braised vegetables.

Opposite: *Every imaginable kind of foodstuff is for sale in this floating market at Damnoen Saduak, south of Bangkok.*

RED CHICKEN CURRY

*The chicken is cooked with a curry paste using red chillies (see below).
It is a fiery hot sauce – for a milder version, reduce the
number of chillies used.*

STEP 2

STEP 3

STEP 4

STEP 5

SERVES 6

4 tbsp vegetable oil
2 garlic cloves, crushed
400 ml/14 fl oz/1³/₄ cups coconut milk
6 chicken breast fillets, skinned and cut into
    bite-sized pieces
125 ml/4 fl oz/¹/₂ cup chicken stock
2 tbsp fish sauce
kaffir lime leaves, sliced red chillies and
    chopped coriander, to garnish

RED CURRY PASTE:

8 dried red chillies, seeded and chopped
2.5 cm/1 in galangal or ginger root, peeled
    and sliced
3 stalks lemon grass, chopped
1 garlic clove, peeled
2 tsp shrimp paste
1 kaffir lime leaf, chopped
1 tsp ground coriander
³/₄ tsp ground cumin
1 tbsp chopped fresh coriander
1 tsp salt and black pepper

1 To make the curry paste, place all
the ingredients in a food processor
or blender and process until smooth.

2 Heat the oil in a large, heavy-based
pan or wok. Add the garlic and
cook for 1 minute or until it turns golden.

3 Stir in the curry paste and cook for
10-15 seconds then gradually add
the coconut milk, stirring constantly
(don't worry if the mixture starts to look
curdled at this stage).

4 Add the chicken pieces and turn in
the sauce mixture to coat. Cook
gently for about 3-5 minutes or until
almost tender.

5 Stir in the chicken stock and fish
sauce, mixing well, then cook for a
further 2 minutes.

6 Transfer to a warmed serving dish
and garnish with lime leaves, sliced
red chillies and chopped coriander. Serve
with rice.

CURRY PASTE

There are two basic curry pastes used in
Thai cuisine – red and green, depending
upon whether they are made from red or
green chilli peppers. The basic paste can
be made and stored in a lidded jar in the
refrigerator for up to 2 weeks.

STEP 2

STEP 3

STEP 4

STEP 5

BARBECUED CHICKEN LEGS

Just the thing to put on the barbecue – chicken legs, coated with a spicy, curry-like butter, then grilled until crispy and golden. Serve with a crisp green seasonal salad and rice.

SERVES 6

12 chicken drumsticks

SPICED BUTTER:
175 g/6 oz/³/₄ cup butter
2 garlic cloves, crushed
1 tsp grated ginger root
2 tsp ground turmeric
4 tsp cayenne pepper
2 tbsp lime juice
3 tbsp mango chutney

1 Prepare a barbecue with medium coals or preheat a conventional grill (broiler) to moderate.

2 To make the Spiced Butter mixture, beat the butter with the garlic, ginger, turmeric, cayenne pepper, lime juice and chutney until it is blended well.

3 Using a sharp knife, slash each chicken leg to the bone 3-4 times.

4 Cook the drumsticks over the barbecue for about 12-15 minutes or until almost cooked. Alternatively, grill (broil) the chicken for about 10-12 minutes until almost cooked, turning halfway through.

5 Spread the chicken legs liberally with the butter mixture and continue to cook for a further 5-6 minutes, turning and basting frequently with the butter until golden and crisp.

6 Serve hot or cold with a crisp green salad and rice.

VARIATION

This spicy butter mixture would be equally effective on grilled chicken or turkey breast fillets. Skin before coating with the mixture.

32

STEP 2

STEP 3

STEP 5a

STEP 5b

ROAST BABY CHICKENS

Poussins, stuffed with lemon grass and lime leaves, coated with a spicy Thai paste, then roasted until crisp and golden, make a wonderful, aromatic dish for a special occasion.

SERVES 4
OVEN: 200°C/400°F/GAS 6

*4 small poussins, weighing about 350-
    500 g/12 oz-1 lb each
coriander leaves and lime wedges, to garnish
a mixture of wild rice and Basmati rice,
    to serve*

MARINADE:
*4 garlic cloves, peeled
2 fresh coriander roots
1 tbsp light soy sauce
salt and pepper*

STUFFING:
*4 blades lemon grass
4 kaffir lime leaves
4 slices ginger root
about 6 tbsp coconut milk, to brush*

1 Wash the chickens and dry on paper towels.

2 Place all the ingredients for the marinade in a small blender and purée until smooth, or grind down in a pestle and mortar. Season to taste with salt and pepper. Rub this marinade mixture into the skin of the chickens, using the back of a spoon to spread it evenly over the skins.

3 Place a blade of lemon grass, a lime leaf and a piece of ginger in the cavity of each chicken.

4 Place the chickens in a roasting pan and brush lightly with the coconut milk. Roast for 30 minutes in the preheated oven.

5 Remove from the oven, brush again with coconut milk, return to the oven and cook for a further 15-25 minutes, until golden and cooked through, depending upon the size of the chickens. The chickens are cooked when the juices from the thigh run clear and are not tinged at all with pink.

6 Serve with the pan juices poured over. Garnish with coriander leaves and lime wedges.

GREEN CHILLI CHICKEN

The green chilli paste gives a hot and spicy flavour to the chicken, which takes on a vibrant green colour.

STEP 2

STEP 3

STEP 4

STEP 5

SERVES 4

5 tbsp vegetable oil
500 g/1 lb boneless chicken breasts, sliced
   into thin strips
50 ml/2 fl oz/¼ cup coconut milk
3 tbsp brown sugar
3 tsp fish sauce
3 tbsp sliced red and green chillies, seeded
4-6 tbsp chopped fresh basil
3 tbsp thick coconut milk or cream
finely chopped fresh chillies, seeded, lemon
   grass and lemon slices, to garnish

GREEN CURRY PASTE:

2 tsp ground ginger
2 tsp ground coriander
2 tsp caraway seeds,
2 tsp ground nutmeg
2 tsp shrimp paste
2 tsp salt
2 tsp black pepper
pinch of ground cloves
1 stalk lemon grass, finely chopped
2 tbsp chopped coriander
2 garlic cloves, peeled
2 onions, peeled
grated rind and juice of 2 limes
4 fresh green chillies, about 5 cm/2 in long,
   seeded

1 To make the curry paste, place all the ingredients and 2 tablespoons of the oil in a food processor or blender and process to a smooth paste.

2 Heat the remaining oil in a heavy-based pan or wok. Add the curry paste and cook for about 30 seconds.

3 Add the chicken strips to the wok and stir-fry over a high heat for about 2-3 minutes.

4 Add the coconut milk, brown sugar, fish sauce and chillies. Cook for 5 minutes, stirring frequently.

5 Remove from the heat, add the basil and toss well to mix.

6 Transfer the chicken to a warmed serving dish. To serve, spoon on a little of the thick coconut milk or cream and garnish with chopped chillies, lemon grass and lemon slices. Serve with steamed or boiled rice.

STEP 1

STEP 2

STEP 3

STEP 4

PEANUT SESAME CHICKEN

In this quickly prepared dish chicken strips are stir-fried with vegetables. Sesame and peanuts give extra crunch and flavour and the fruit juice glaze gives a lovely shiny coating to the sauce.

SERVES 4

2 tbsp vegetable oil
2 tbsp sesame oil
500g/1 lb boneless, skinned chicken breasts, sliced into strips
250 g/8 oz broccoli, divided into small florets
250 g/8 oz baby or dwarf corn, halved if large
1 small red (bell) pepper, cored, seeded and sliced
2 tbsp soy sauce
250 ml/8 fl oz/1 cup orange juice
2 tsp cornflour (cornstarch)
2 tbsp toasted sesame seeds
60 g/2 oz/⅓ cup roasted, shelled, unsalted peanuts

1 Heat the oils in a large, heavy-based frying pan or wok, add the chicken strips and stir-fry until browned, about 4-5 minutes.

2 Add the broccoli, corn and red (bell) pepper and stir-fry for a further 1-2 minutes.

3 Meanwhile, mix the soy sauce with the orange juice and cornflour (cornstarch). Stir into the chicken and vegetable mixture, stirring constantly until the sauce has slightly thickened and a glaze develops.

4 Stir in the sesame seeds and peanuts, mixing well. Heat for a further 3-4 minutes then serve at once, with rice or noodles.

PEANUTS

Make sure you use the unsalted variety of peanuts or the dish will be too salty, as the soy sauce adds saltiness.

CHICKEN & NOODLE ONE-POT

Flavoursome chicken and vegetables cooked with Chinese egg noodles in a coconut sauce. Serve in deep soup bowls.

STEP 1

SERVES 4

1 tbsp sunflower oil
1 onion, sliced
1 garlic clove, crushed
2.5 cm/1 in root ginger, peeled and grated
1 bunch spring onions (scallions), sliced
   diagonally
500 g/1 lb chicken breast fillet, skinned and
   cut into bite-sized pieces
2 tbsp mild curry paste
475 ml/16 fl oz/2 cups coconut milk
300 ml/¹/₂ pint/1¹/₄ cups chicken stock
250 g/8 oz Chinese egg noodles
2 tsp lime juice
salt and pepper
basil sprigs, to garnish

1 Heat the oil in a wok or large, heavy-based pan. Add the onion, garlic, ginger and spring onions (scallions) and stir-fry for 2 minutes until softened.

2 Add the chicken pieces and curry paste and stir-fry until the vegetables and chicken are golden brown, about 4 minutes.

3 Stir in the coconut milk, stock and salt and pepper to taste, mixing until well blended.

4 Bring to the boil, break the noodles into large pieces, if necessary, add to the pan, cover and simmer for about 6-8 minutes until the noodles are just tender, stirring occasionally.

5 Add the lime juice, taste and adjust the seasoning, if necessary, then serve at once in deep soup bowls.

STEP 2

STEP 3

STEP 4

COOK'S TIP

If you enjoy the hot flavours of Thai cooking then substitute the mild curry paste in the above recipe with Thai hot curry paste (found in most supermarkets) but reduce the quantity to 1 tablespoon.

DUCK WITH GINGER & LIME

Just the thing for a lazy summer day – roasted duck breasts sliced and served with a dressing made of ginger, lime juice, sesame oil and fish sauce. Serve on a bed of assorted fresh salad leaves in season.

STEP 1a

SERVES 6
OVEN: 200°C/400°F/GAS 6

*3 boneless Barbary duck breasts, about
   250 g/8 oz each
salt*

DRESSING:
*125 ml/4 fl oz/¹/₂ cup olive oil
2 tsp sesame oil
2 tbsp lime juice
grated rind and juice of 1 orange
2 tsp fish sauce
1 tbsp grated ginger root
1 garlic clove, crushed
2 tsp light soy sauce
3 spring onions (scallions), finely chopped
1 tsp sugar
about 250 g/8 oz assorted salad leaves
orange slices, to garnish, optional*

STEP 1b

1 Wash the duck breasts, dry on paper towels, then cut in half. Prick the skin all over with a fork and season well with salt. Place the duck pieces, skin-side down, on a wire rack or trivet over a roasting tin. Cook the duck in the preheated oven for 10 minutes, then turn over and cook for a further 12-15 minutes, or until the duck is cooked, but still pink in the centre, and the skin is crisp.

2 To make the dressing, beat the oils with the lime juice, orange rind and juice, fish sauce, ginger, garlic, soy sauce, spring onions (scallions) and sugar until well blended.

3 Remove the duck from the oven, allow to cool, then cut into thick slices. Add a little of the dressing to moisten and coat the duck.

4 To serve, arrange assorted salad leaves on a serving dish. Top with the sliced duck breasts and drizzle with the remaining salad dressing.

5 Garnish with orange twists, if using, then serve at once.

STEP 2

COOK'S TIP

If an extra crisp skin is preferred on the duck then quickly fry the duck breasts, skin-side down, in a non-stick pan (without any additional oil) for a few minutes until golden. Cook in the oven as above, but reduce the cooking time by about 3 minutes.

STEP 3

STEP 1

STEP 2

STEP 3a

STEP 3b

BEEF & BOK CHOY

A colourful selection of vegetables stir-fried with tender strips of steak.

SERVES 4

*1 large head of bok choy, about 250-
275 g/ 8-9 oz, torn into large pieces*
2 tbsp vegetable oil
2 garlic cloves, crushed
*500 g/ 1 lb rump or fillet steak, cut into thin
strips*
*150 g/ 5 oz mangetout (snow peas),
trimmed*
150 g/ 5 oz baby or dwarf corn
6 spring onions (scallions), chopped
*2 red (bell) peppers, cored, seeded and thinly
sliced*
2 tbsp oyster sauce
1 tbsp fish sauce
1 tbsp sugar

1 Steam the bok choy leaves over
boiling water until just tender.
Keep warm.

2 Heat the oil in a large, heavy-based
frying pan or wok, add the garlic
and steak strips and stir-fry until just
browned, about 1-2 minutes.

3 Add the mangetout (snow peas),
baby corn, spring onions
(scallions), red (bell) pepper, oyster
sauce, fish sauce and sugar to the pan,
mixing well. Stir-fry for a further 2-3

minutes until the vegetables are just
tender, but still crisp.

4 Arrange the bok choy leaves in the
base of a heated serving dish and
spoon the beef and vegetable mixture
into the centre.

5 Serve the stir-fry immediately,
with rice or noodles.

VARIATION

Bok choy is one of the most important
ingredients in this dish. If unavailable, use
Chinese leaves, kai choy (mustard leaves)
or pak choy.

GREEN BEEF CURRY

This is a quickly-made curry prepared with strips of beef steak, cubed aubergine (eggplant) and onion in a cream sauce flavoured with green curry paste. Serve with fluffy rice and a salad.

STEP 1

SERVES 4

1 aubergine (eggplant), peeled and cubed
2 onions, cut into thin wedges
2 tbsp vegetable oil
Green Curry Paste (see page 37)
500 g/1 lb beef fillet, cut into thin strips
475 ml/16 fl oz/2 cups thick coconut milk
  or cream
2 tbsp fish sauce
1 tbsp brown sugar
1 red chilli, seeded and very finely chopped
1 green chilli, seeded and very finely chopped
2.5 cm/1 in ginger root, finely chopped
4 kaffir lime leaves, torn into pieces
chopped fresh basil, to garnish

1 Blanch the aubergine (eggplant) cubes and onion wedges in boiling water for about 2 minutes, to soften. Drain thoroughly.

2 Heat the oil in a large heavy-based pan or wok, add the curry paste and cook for 1 minute.

3 Add the beef strips and stir-fry, over a high heat, for about 1 minute, to brown on all sides.

4 Add the coconut milk or cream, fish sauce and sugar to the pan and bring the mixture to the boil, stirring constantly.

5 Add the aubergine (eggplant) and onion, chillies, ginger and lime leaves. Cook for a further 2 minutes.

6 Sprinkle with chopped basil to serve. Accompany with rice.

STEP 2

COCONUT MILK

Coconut milk is sold in cans, or you can make your own. Pour 300 ml/½ pint/1¼ cups boiling water over 250 g/8 oz shredded coconut and simmer over low heat for 30 minutes. Strain the milk into a bowl through a piece of muslin. Gather the ends of muslin together and squeeze tightly to extract as much liquid as possible.

STEP 3

STEP 4

PEPPERED BEEF CASHEW

A simple but stunning dish of tender strips of beef mixed with crunchy cashew nuts, coated in a hot sauce. Serve with rice noodles.

STEP 1

STEP 2

STEP 4

STEP 5

SERVES 4

1 tbsp groundnut or sunflower oil
1 tbsp sesame oil
1 onion, sliced
1 garlic clove, crushed
1 tbsp grated ginger root
500 g/1 lb fillet or rump steak, cut into thin
    strips
2 tsp palm or demerara sugar
2 tbsp light soy sauce
1 small yellow (bell) pepper, cored, seeded
    and sliced
1 red (bell) pepper, cored, seeded and sliced
4 spring onions (scallions), chopped
2 celery sticks, chopped
4 large open-cap mushrooms, sliced
4 tbsp roasted cashew nuts
3 tbsp stock or white wine

1 Heat the oils in a large, heavy-based frying pan or wok. Add the onion, garlic and ginger and stir-fry for about 2 minutes until softened and lightly coloured.

2 Add the steak strips and stir-fry for a further 2-3 minutes, until the meat has browned.

3 Add the sugar and soy sauce, mixing well.

4 Add the (bell) peppers, spring onions (scallions), celery, mushrooms and cashews, mixing well.

5 Add the stock or wine and stir-fry for 2-3 minutes until the beef is cooked through and the vegetables are tender-crisp.

6 Serve the stir-fry immediately with rice noodles.

PALM SUGAR

Palm sugar is a thick brown sugar with a slightly caramel taste. It is sold in cakes, or in small containers. If not available, use soft dark brown or demerara sugar.

GARLIC PORK & SHRIMPS

This is a wonderful one-pot dish of stir-fried pork fillet with shrimps and noodles that is made in minutes. Serve straight from the pan.

STEP 1

SERVES 4

250 g/8 oz packet medium egg noodles
3 tbsp vegetable oil
2 garlic cloves, crushed
350 g/12 oz pork fillet, cut into strips
4 tbsp/⅓ cup dried shrimps, or 125 g/4 oz
    peeled prawns (shrimp)
1 bunch spring onions (scallions), finely
    chopped
90 g/3 oz/¾ cup chopped roasted and
    shelled unsalted peanuts
3 tbsp fish sauce
1½ tsp palm or demerara sugar
1-2 small red chillies, seeded and finely
    chopped (to taste)
3 tbsp lime juice
3 tbsp chopped fresh coriander
coriander sprigs, to garnish

1 Place the noodles in a large pan of boiling water, then immediately remove from the heat. Cover and leave to stand for 6 minutes, stirring once halfway through the time. At the end of 5 minutes the noodles will be perfectly cooked. Alternatively, follow the packet instructions. Drain the noodles thoroughly and keep warm.

2 Heat the oil in a large, heavy-based pan or wok, add the garlic and pork and stir-fry until the pork strips are browned, about 2-3 minutes.

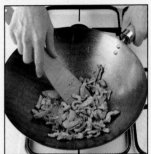

STEP 2

3 Add the dried shrimps or shelled prawns (shrimp), spring onions (scallions), peanuts, fish sauce, sugar, chillies to taste and lime juice. Stir-fry for a further 1 minute.

4 Add the cooked noodles and coriander and stir-fry until heated through, about 1 minute. Serve the stir-fry immediately, garnished with coriander sprigs. If you prefer, the dish can be prepared with rice as an accompaniment rather than adding in the noodles.

STEP 3

FISH SAUCE

Fish sauce is made from pressed, salted fish and is widely available in super-markets and oriental stores. It is very salty, so no extra salt should be added.

STEP 4

CHAPTER FOUR

Accompaniments

Good Thai food is a happy marriage of many different dishes that contrast in flavour, colour and texture. Rice may well be the staple food, but freshly-cooked plain long-grain rice is only one way of serving this basic. In countless other dishes it is baked, steamed, stir-fried and boiled with an almost infinite spectrum of vegetables, herbs, spices and flavourings to entice and delight.

Noodles too have a major role to play when snacks come to the fore. Many noodles, fried with just a few extra ingredients, make superb light meals to enjoy in their own right. No self-respecting Thai would do without the bowl of mid-day noodles!

The Thais also employ clever ways with their rich supply of vegetables such as shallots, garlic, baby corn, cabbage, green beans, broccoli, (bell) peppers and mushrooms. Sliced and diced they are used in imaginative stir-fries; cubed and sliced they are braised in aromatic broths and sauces; and finely shredded they make exciting, palate-tingling salads with exotic dressings using limes, fish sauce, ginger, soy sauce and sesame oil.

Opposite: *A basket stall in the floating market in Bangkok.*

THAI SALAD

This is a typical Thai-style salad made by mixing fruit and vegetables with the sharp, sweet and fishy flavours of the dressing.

STEP 1

SERVES 4-6

250 g/8 oz white cabbage, finely shredded
2 tomatoes, skinned, seeded and chopped
250 g/8 oz cooked green beans, halved if large
125 g/4 oz peeled prawns (shrimp)
1 papaya, peeled, seeded and chopped
1-2 fresh red chillies, seeded and very finely sliced
60 g/2 oz/scant ⅓ cup roasted salted peanuts, crushed
handful of lettuce or baby spinach leaves, shredded or torn into small pieces

DRESSING:
4 tbsp lime juice
2 tbsp fish sauce
sugar, to taste
pepper
coriander sprigs, to garnish

1 Mix the cabbage with the tomatoes, green beans, prawns (shrimp), three-quarters of the papaya and half the chillies in a bowl. Stir in two-thirds of the crushed peanuts and mix well.

2 Line the rim of a large serving plate with the lettuce or spinach and pile the salad mixture into the centre.

3 To make the dressing, beat the lime juice with the fish sauce and add sugar and pepper to taste. Drizzle over the salad.

4 Scatter the top with the remaining papaya, chillies and crushed peanuts. Garnish with coriander leaves and serve at once.

STEP 2

STEP 3

SKINNING TOMATOES

To skin tomatoes, make a cross at the base with a very sharp knife, then immerse in a bowl of boiling water for a few minutes. Remove with a slotted spoon and peel off the skin.

STEP 4

THAI FRAGRANT COCONUT RICE

This is the finest rice to serve with Thai-style food. Basmati rice is cooked with creamed coconut, lemon grass, fresh ginger and spices to make a wonderfully aromatic, fluffy rice.

STEP 1

SERVES **4-6**

2.5 cm/1 in piece ginger root, peeled and
   sliced
2 cloves
1 piece lemon grass, bruised and halved
2 tsp ground nutmeg
1 cinnamon stick
1 bay leaf
2 small thin strips lime zest
1 tsp salt
30 g/1 oz creamed coconut, chopped
600 ml/1 pint/2¹/₂ cups water
350 g/12 oz/1³/₄ cups basmati rice
ground pepper

1 Place the ginger, cloves, lemon grass, nutmeg, cinnamon stick, bay leaf, lime zest, salt, creamed coconut and water in a large, heavy-based pan and bring slowly to the boil.

2 Add the rice, stir well, then cover and simmer, over a very gentle heat, for about 15 minutes or until all the liquid has been absorbed and the rice is tender but still has a bite to it.

3 Remove from the heat, add pepper to taste, then fluff up the rice with a fork. Remove the large pieces of spices before serving.

LEMON GRASS

When using a whole stem of lemon grass (rather than chopped lemon grass), beat it well to bruise it so that the flavour is fully released. Lemon zest or a pared piece of lemon peel can be used instead.

STEP 2a

STEP 2b

COOKING RICE

An alternative method of cooking the rice – the absorption method – leaves you free to concentrate on other dishes. Add the rice to the pan as in step 1, then bring back to the boil. Stir well, then cover tightly and turn off the heat. Leave for 20-25 minutes before removing the lid – the rice will be perfectly cooked.

STEP 3

SESAME HOT NOODLES

Plain egg noodles are all the better when tossed in a dressing made with nutty sesame oil, soy sauce, peanut butter, coriander, lime juice, chilli and sesame seeds. Serve hot as a main meal accompaniment.

STEP 1

SERVES 6

2 x 250 g/8 oz pkts medium egg noodles
3 tbsp sunflower oil
2 tbsp sesame oil
1 garlic clove, crushed
1 tbsp smooth peanut butter
1 small green chilli, seeded and very finely
   chopped
3 tbsp toasted sesame seeds
4 tbsp light soy sauce
1-2 tbsp lime juice
salt and pepper
4 tbsp chopped fresh coriander

1 Place the noodles in a large pan of boiling water, then immediately remove from the heat. Cover and leave to stand for 6 minutes, stirring once halfway through the time. At the end of 6 minutes the noodles will be perfectly cooked. Otherwise follow packet instructions.

2 Meanwhile, to make the dressing, mix the oils with the garlic and peanut butter until smooth.

3 Add the chilli, sesame seeds, soy sauce and lime juice, according to taste and mix well. Season with salt and pepper.

4 Drain the noodles thoroughly then place in a heated serving bowl. Add the dressing and coriander and toss well to mix. Serve immediately.

STEP 2

STEP 3

COOKING NOODLES

If you are cooking noodles ahead of time, toss the cooked, drained noodles in 2 teaspoons sesame oil, then turn into a bowl. Cover and keep warm.

STEP 4

STEP 2

STEP 3

STEP 4a

STEP 4b

THAI FRIED RICE

*The Thais often serve their rice fried, but not just plain and simple –
they give theirs an extra punch and bit of a zip with hot red chillies,
spring onions (scallions) and fish sauce.*

SERVES 4

250 g/8 oz/1 cup Basmati rice
3 tbsp sunflower oil
1 hot red chilli, seeded and finely chopped
2 tsp fish sauce
3 spring onions (scallions) chopped
1 large egg (size 1), beaten
1 tbsp chopped parsley or coriander
1 tbsp soy sauce
1 tsp sugar
salt and pepper

1 Cook the rice in boiling salted water until tender, about 10 minutes. Drain, rinse with boiling water and drain again thoroughly. Spread out on a large plate or baking sheet to dry.

2 Heat the oil in a large, heavy-based frying pan or wok until hot. Add the chilli, fish sauce and spring onions (scallions) and stir-fry for 1-2 minutes.

3 Add the beaten egg and stir-fry quickly so that the egg scrambles into small fluffy pieces.

4 Fork through the rice to separate the grains, then add to the pan and stir-fry for about 1 minute to mix and heat through.

5 Sprinkle a little of the chopped parsley over the rice. Mix the soy sauce with the sugar and remaining chopped parsley and stir into the rice mixture, tossing well to mix. Serve immediately.

FRIED RICE

For perfect fried rice it is important that the rice is thoroughly dry and cold before it is added to the pan, otherwise it may become lumpy and soggy.

THAI BRAISED VEGETABLES

This colourful selection of braised vegetables makes a splendid accompaniment to a main dish.

STEP 1

STEP 2

STEP 3

STEP 5

SERVES 4-6

3 tbsp sunflower oil

1 garlic clove, crushed

1 Chinese cabbage, thickly shredded

2 onions, peeled and cut into wedges

250 g/8 oz broccoli florets

2 large carrots, peeled and cut into thin julienne strips

12 baby or dwarf corn, halved if large

50 g/2 oz mangetout (snow peas), halved

90 g/3 oz Chinese or oyster mushrooms, sliced

1 tbsp grated ginger root

175 ml/6 fl oz/³/₄ cup vegetable stock

2 tbsp light soy sauce

1 tbsp cornflour (cornstarch)

salt and pepper

¹/₂ tsp sugar

1 Heat the oil in a large, heavy-based frying pan or wok. Add the garlic, cabbage, onions, broccoli, carrots, corn, mangetout (snow peas), mushrooms and ginger and stir-fry for 2 minutes.

2 Add the stock, cover and cook for a further 2-3 minutes.

3 Blend the soy sauce with the cornflour (cornstarch) and salt and pepper to taste.

4 Remove the braised vegetables from the pan with a slotted spoon and keep warm. Add the soy sauce mixture to the pan juices, mixing well. Bring to the boil, stirring constantly, until the mixture thickens slightly. Stir in the sugar.

5 Return the vegetables to the pan and toss in the slightly thickened sauce. Cook gently to just heat through then serve immediately.

VARIATION

This dish also makes an ideal vegetarian main meal. Double the quantities, to serve 4-6, and serve with noodles or Thai Fried Rice (page 60).

CHAPTER FIVE

Desserts

Few things are more beguiling and enticing than a stunning array of mixed tropical fruits carefully arranged on a platter to round off a meal, and the Thais make this traditional dessert an art form: slices of sunset-coloured mango and papaya nestle against jewel-like green and black discs of kiwi fruit, wheels of fragrant yellow pineapple and diagonally sliced strips of banana.

Desserts, as we know them, usually only appear at banquets and special festive occasions, although sweet treats can be bought ready-made by street vendors on almost every corner.

When it is time to celebrate the Thais use their wealth of tropical fruits to make superb fruit salads, stuffed pancakes, wontons and baby dumplings. They use rice to make a rich and creamy pudding baked with coconut milk, and purée fruits to make ice-creams, parfaits and exotic water ices. The all-time favourite is Thai-style Bananas, sliced and cooked in butter with orange zest, sugar and lime juice, flamed with orange-flavoured liqueur and sprinkled with toasted coconut shreds, all the better for serving with a dollop of coconut-flavoured cream or ice-cream. No wonder the Thais save it for best!

Opposite: *A street vendor in Bangkok displays her fruit on banana leaves, often used to wrap and bake fish.*

THAI-STYLE BANANAS

The Thais rarely finish a meal with an elaborate dessert, preferring to eat a selection of tropical fruits. This is one of the exceptions and you can understand why.

SERVES 6

3 tbsp shredded fresh coconut
50 g/2 oz/¼ cup unsalted butter
1 tbsp grated ginger root
grated zest of 1 orange
5 bananas
50 g/2 oz/¼ cup caster sugar
4 tbsp fresh lime juice
5 tbsp orange liqueur (Cointreau or Grand Marnier, for example)
3 tsp toasted sesame seeds
lime slices, to decorate
ice-cream, to serve (optional)

1 Heat a small non-stick frying pan until hot. Add the coconut and cook, stirring constantly, for about 1 minute until lightly coloured. Remove from the pan and allow to cool.

2 Heat the butter in a large frying pan until it melts. Add the ginger and orange zest and mix well.

3 Peel and slice the bananas lengthways (and halve if they are very large). Place the bananas cut-side down in the butter mixture and cook for 1-2 minutes or until the sauce mixture starts to become sticky. Turn to coat in the sauce.

4 Remove the bananas from the pan and place on heated serving plates. Keep warm.

5 Return the pan to the heat and add the orange liqueur, stirring well to blend. Ignite with a taper, allow the flames to die down, then pour over the bananas.

6 Sprinkle with the coconut and sesame seeds and serve at once, decorated with slices of lime.

VARIATION

For a very special treat try serving with a flavoured ice-cream such as coconut, ginger or praline.

STEP 1

STEP 2

STEP 3

STEP 5

STEP 1

STEP 3a

STEP 3b

STEP 5

MANGO PARFAIT

This is a beautifully soft parfait that can be served straight from the freezer. Serve with crisp dessert biscuits or, when time and the waistline allows, with deep-fried, sugar-dusted wontons.

SERVES 4

1 large ripe mango
juice of 1 lime
about 1 tbsp caster sugar
3 egg yolks
60 g/2 oz/½ cup icing (confectioner's)
    sugar, sifted
150 ml/¼ pint/⅔ cup double (heavy)
    cream
lime zest, to decorate
fried wontons dusted with sugar, to serve
    (optional)

1 Peel the mango and slice the flesh away from the stone. Purée in a food processor or blender with the lime juice and caster sugar to taste, until the mixture is smooth.

2 Beat the egg yolks with the icing (confectioner's) sugar until the mixture is pale and thick, then fold in the mango purée.

3 Whip the cream until it stands in soft peaks. Fold into the mango mixture with a metal spoon.

4 Pour the mango mixture into 4 freezerproof serving glasses and freeze until firm, about 4-6 hours.

5 Serve the parfaits straight from the freezer (they will be soft enough to scoop) with crisp dessert biscuits or warm fried wontons (see instructions below) dusted with sugar.

FRIED WONTONS

Allow about 2 wontons per person. Deep-fry the wonton skins in hot oil for about 30 seconds until crisp and golden. Drain on paper towels, then dust with icing (confectioner's) sugar to serve.

STEP 1

STEP 2

STEP 3a

STEP 3b

BAKED COCONUT RICE PUDDING

A wonderful baked rice pudding cooked with flavoursome coconut milk and a little lime rind. Serve hot or chilled with fresh or stewed fruit.

SERVES 4-6
OVEN: 170°C / 325°F / GAS 2

90 g / 3 oz / scant ⅓ cup short or round-grain pudding rice
600 ml / 1 pint / 2½ cups coconut milk
300 ml / ½ pint / 1¼ cups milk
1 large strip lime rind
60 g / 2 oz / ¼ cup caster sugar
knob of butter
pinch of ground star anise (optional)
fresh or stewed fruit, to serve

1 Mix the rice with the coconut milk, milk, lime rind and sugar.

2 Pour the rice mixture into a lightly-greased 1.4 litre / 2½ pint shallow ovenproof dish and dot the surface with a little butter. Bake in the oven for about 30 minutes.

3 Remove and discard the strip of lime. Stir the pudding well, add the pinch of ground star anise, if using, return to the oven and cook for a further 1-2 hours or until almost all the milk has been absorbed and a golden brown skin has baked on the top of the pudding. Cover the top of the pudding with foil if it starts to brown too much towards the end of the cooking time.

4 Serve the pudding warm or chilled with fresh or stewed fruit.

COOK'S TIP

As the mixture cools it thickens. If you plan to serve the rice chilled then fold in about 3 tbsp cream or extra coconut milk before serving to give a thinner consistency.

STEP 1

STEP 2a

STEP 2b

STEP 5

FRUIT SALAD WITH GINGER SYRUP

This is a very special fruit salad made from the most exotic and colourful fruits that are soaked in a syrup made with fresh ginger and ginger wine.

SERVES 6-8

2.5 cm/1 in ginger root, peeled and chopped
60 g/2 oz/¼ cup caster sugar
150 ml/¼ pint/²⁄₃ cup water
grated rind and juice of 1 lime
4 tbsp/¹⁄₃ cup ginger wine
1 fresh pineapple, peeled, cored and cut into
   bite-sized pieces
2 ripe mangoes, peeled, stoned and diced
4 kiwi fruit, peeled and sliced
1 papaya, peeled, seeded and diced
2 passion fruit, halved and flesh removed
350 g/12 oz lychees, peeled and stoned
¼ fresh coconut, grated
60 g/2 oz Cape gooseberries, to decorate
   (optional)
coconut ice-cream, to serve (optional)

1 Place the ginger, sugar, water and lime juice in a small pan and bring slowly to the boil. Simmer for 1 minute, remove from the heat and allow the syrup to cool slightly.

2 Pass the sugar syrup through a fine sieve then add the ginger wine and mix well. Allow to cool completely.

3 Place the prepared pineapple, mango, kiwi, papaya, passion fruit and lychees in a serving bowl. Add the cold syrup and mix well. Cover and chill for 2-4 hours.

4 Just before serving, add half of the grated coconut to the salad and mix well. Sprinkle the remainder on the top of the fruit salad.

5 If using Cape gooseberries to decorate the fruit salad, peel back each calyx to form a flower. Wipe the berries with a damp cloth, then arrange them around the side of the fruit salad before serving.

PANCAKES POLAMAI

These Thai pancakes are filled with an exotic array of tropical fruits.
Decorate lavishly with tropical flowers or mint sprigs.

STEP 1

Serves 4

BATTER:
125 g/4 oz/1 cup plain flour
pinch of salt
1 egg
1 egg yolk
300 ml/½ pint/1¼ cups coconut milk
4 tsp vegetable oil, plus oil for frying

FILLING:
1 banana
1 papaya
juice of 1 lime
2 passion fruit
1 mango, peeled, stoned and sliced
4 lychees, stoned and halved
1-2 tbsp honey
flowers or mint sprigs, to decorate

1 To make the batter, sift the flour into a bowl with the salt. Make a well in the centre, add the egg and egg yolk and a little of the coconut milk. Gradually draw the flour into the egg mixture, beating well and gradually adding the remaining coconut milk to make a smooth batter. Add the oil and mix well. Cover and chill for 30 minutes.

2 To make the filling, peel and slice the banana and place in a bowl.

Peel and slice the papaya, remove and discard the seeds then cut into bite-sized chunks. Add to the banana with the lime juice and mix well to coat.

STEP 2

3 Cut the passion fruit in half and scoop out the flesh and seeds into the fruit bowl. Add the mango, lychees and honey and mix well.

4 To make the pancakes, heat a little oil in a 15 cm/6 inch crêpe or frying pan. Pour in just enough of the pancake batter to cover the base of the pan and tilt so that it spreads thinly and evenly. Cook until the pancake is just set and the underside is lightly browned, turn and briefly cook the other side. Remove from the pan and keep warm. Repeat with the remaining batter to make a total of 8 pancakes.

STEP 3

5 To serve, place a little of the prepared fruit filling along the centre of each pancake and then, using both hands, roll it into a cone shape. Lay seam-side down on warmed serving plates, allowing 2 pancakes per serving.

6 Serve the stuffed pancakes at once, decorated with flowers and mint sprigs, if liked.

STEP 4

THAI COOKING

COOKING EQUIPMENT AND METHODS

In Thailand, there are few gas and electric ovens or grills as Westerners know them, most cooking being done on an open charcoal stove. Meat and fish are frequently barbecued or grilled and woks are set upon their surfaces to stir-fry, boil, steam or simmer dishes. A wok is therefore the most necessary piece of equipment required for cooking - although a heavy-duty, deep frying pan may suffice. There is really very little need for specialist equipment although the following special items may be worth the investment to the avid Thai cook:

Pestle and Mortar An absolute must to crush spices, herbs and other flavourings to make pastes for flavouring a whole host of dishes. A small electric herb grinder or coffee grinder, specifically reserved for spices, could be employed instead and it does cut down on the elbow grease!

Steamer A steamer, with a good tight-fitting lid, is necessary to cook foods gently above boiling water. Chinese bamboo steamers are ideal solutions at very little cost and can be purchased cheaply from Chinese supermarkets. An improvised set-up could use a metal colander over a saucepan with tight-fitting lid to cover.

continued opposite

Thailand has a richly abundant and totally unique cuisine that has changed little over the centuries, despite regular foreign intervention. Today, it still stands independent, with head held high, to critical gastronomic scrutiny and fares the better for it.

It is not difficult to spot the influence of near neighbours like China and India in stir-fries and curries but somehow they are given the unmistakeable Thai treatment with herbs, spices and coconut milk. So it is easy to see how on the one hand Thai cuisine can be described as light, aromatic and zestful, yet on the other hot, handsome, robust and full-blooded!

Thai cuisine is dependent upon the rich harvests of rice, green vegetables, herbs, spices and fruit. A lavish supply of fish means that normally at least one fish dish, be it sizzled prawns (shrimp), a fish curry or banana-wrapped baked whole fish, features in every Thai meal. Meat, of all types, also makes for a varied cuisine where there are few, if any, religious restrictions to the basic diet.

Rice is the staple food and is served at every meal with many main-course meat, fish, poultry and vegetable dishes in a sauce. Noodles are generally served as snack or "fast" foods to supplement the main meal. Soups also feature frequently and are typically flavoured with Thai staples like lemon grass, lime juice and fish sauce.

Creamy curries, ranging from mild and aromatic to fierce and fiery, are prepared daily with care from some of the finest fresh ingredients and spicy curry pastes whose bases are red or green chilli peppers.

SPECIAL INGREDIENTS

Such has been the popularity of Thai food that nearly every supermarket boasts the ingredients required to cook a Thai meal. Only a few special foods will have to be purchased from specialist and oriental food stores and, fortunately, every town now seems to have at least one good supplier.

Bamboo Shoots Still only available canned and sometimes dried (which need soaking before use), bamboo shoots are the crunchy cream-coloured shoots of the bamboo plant.

Banana Leaves These are the large green inedible leaves of the banana tree that are principally used for wrapping food and for making containers for steaming purposes. They give the food a slightly aromatic delicate flavour but cannot be eaten.

Basil Holy basil or Thai basil, available from specialist stores, has a stronger, more pungent and sharper flavour than our domestic or "sweet" basil. When unavailable use ordinary basil in the same proportions.

Bean Sauce A thick sauce made from yellow or black soy beans. The crushed beans are mixed with flour, vinegar, spices and salt to make a spicy, sometimes salty and definitely aromatic sauce. It is usually sold in cans or jars.

Bean Sprouts The tiny, crunchy shoots of mung beans. These are widely available fresh and should be used on the day of purchase. Canned beansprouts are available but generally lack flavour and crunchiness.

Chilli Paste This is a paste of roast ground chillies mixed with oil. Depending upon the chillies used, the colour and flavour will differ appreciably so only add a small amount to err on the side of safety. It is sold in small jars and may be called "Ground Chillies in Oil". A small jar will last a long time if stored in the refrigerator.

Fresh Chillies Fresh chillies come in varying degrees of hotness. Cooking helps to mellow the flavour but a degree of caution should be exercised when using them. If you do not like your food too hot then discard the seeds when you prepare them. Remember, at all costs, to make sure that you wash your hands thoroughly after touching them as they contain an irritant which will sting the eyes and mouth harshly on contact. Fresh chopped hot chillies can be replaced with chilli paste or cayenne pepper but the result will be slightly different. As a general guide for buying - the smaller the chilli the hotter it will be. Most supermarkets stock the larger, milder chilli and this is perhaps the best starting point for the novice Thai cook.

Dried Chillies These add a surprisingly good kick to a dish, especially if they are tossed in oil with other spices at the beginning of cooking. Generally the chillies are added whole but can sometimes be halved. In most cases they should be removed from the dish before serving. Again, the smaller the dried chilli, the hotter the flavour.

Coconut The coconut is used in a good many sweet and savoury Thai dishes and is infinitely better to use than desiccated coconut. Many supermarkets now stock them fresh at little cost.

Coconut Milk Coconut milk is an infusion used to flavour and thicken many Thai dishes. Perhaps the best and easiest type to use comes in cans from Oriental stores but remember to check that it is unsweetened for savoury dishes.

Coriander This is a delicate and fragrant herb that is widely used in Thai cooking. The roots and the leaves are used, the former having a more intense flavour. The roots are generally used for cooking and the leaves are used more for flavouring the cooked and finished dish. Chopped leaves are frequently stirred into a cooked dish or scattered over the surface just prior to serving.

Curry Leaves Rather like bay leaves but not quite so thick and luscious, these are highly aromatic leaves that are chopped, torn or left whole and added to many Thai curries and slow-simmered dishes. Olive-green in colour they can be bought fresh or dried from specialist shops.

Cooking Equipment & Methods cont.
Wok A large frying pan can be used instead of this special pan with distinctive sloping and rounded edges, but devotees will tell you how useful it is not only for stir-frying but also for deep-frying, steaming, boiling, pan-grilling and stewing foods.

PREPARING A FRESH COCONUT

When buying a coconut choose one that is heavy for its size. To open it, pierce the "eyes" with a skewer and pour away the liquid. Heating the coconut in the oven will help with further preparation - place in a preheated moderately hot oven, 190°C/ 375°F/ Gas 5, for about 10-15 minutes, then place on the floor or a sturdy surface and give it a sharp tap with a mallet or hammer. The coconut should cleanly break in two. The flesh can then be prised away with a sharp knife from the shell. The brown skin can then be peeled from the white flesh. Cut the flesh into pieces or grate as required, by hand or in a food processor to use as required. Grated fresh coconut and coconut pieces freeze well for up to 2 months.

FRESH COCONUT MILK

To make it from fresh grated coconut, place about 250 g/8 oz grated coconut in a bowl, pour over about 600 ml/1 pint of boiling water to just cover and leave to stand for 1 hour. Strain through muslin, squeezing hard to extract as much 'thick' milk as possible. If you require coconut cream then leave to stand then skim the 'cream' from the surface for use. Unsweetened dessicated coconut can also be used in the same quantities.

TAMARIND WATER

Tamarind is the dried fruit of the tamarind tree that has a sharp, acidic taste. The pods are used as a souring agent. Sold as pods or pulp they must be made into tamarind water to use. To do this you have to soak 30 g/1 oz pulp in 300 ml/½ pint hot water, stir well and leave for about 20 minutes. The water is then strained off, pressing as much as possible from the pulp. Tamarind paste or concentrate is available from specialist stores and is ready to use. It is simply mixed with stock or water or added directly to the dish. Use according to the packet or recipe instructions. Vinegar or lemon juice in water can be used instead but they make a poor alternative. Tamarind is one of the ingredients that gives Thai cuisine its special sweet and sour flavour.

Fish Paste This is a thick fish paste made from fermented fish or shrimps and salt. It is used only in small amounts since it has enormous flavouring power. Anchovy paste makes a good if not authentic alternative.

Fish Sauce/Nam Pla This is a thin, brown salty sauce that is widely used in Thai cooking instead of salt. It is made by pressing salted fish and is available in many Oriental food stores. There is really no good available substitute so is worth hunting for.

Galangal Galangal is a spice very similar to ginger and is used to replace the latter in Thai cuisine. It can be bought fresh from Oriental food stores but is also available dried and as a powder. The fresh root, which is not as pungent as ginger, needs to be peeled before slicing to use whilst dried pieces need to be soaked in water before using and discarded from the dish before serving. If fresh galangal is unavailable for a recipe then substitute 1 dried slice or 1 teaspoon powder for each 1.5 cm/½ in fresh.

Ginger Root Root ginger is also often used in Thai cooking. Always peel before using then chop, grate or purée to a paste to use. Buy root ginger in small quantities to ensure freshness and store in a plastic bag in the refrigerator.

Kaffir Lime Leaves These are dark green, glossy leaves that have a lemony-lime flavour that can be bought from specialist shops either fresh or dried. Fresh leaves impart the most delicious flavour to a dish so are worth seeking out. Most recipes call for the leaves to be left whole or shredded. This is best done with a pair of scissors. When stocks cannot be found then substitute 1 leaf with about 1 teaspoon finely grated lime zest.

Lemon Grass Known also as citronelle, lemon grass is a tropical grass with a pungent, aromatic lemon flavour. It is fairly easy to buy fresh from supermarkets. When chopped lemon grass is specified then use the thick bulk end of the spring onion (scallions) like stem. Alternatively, if the whole stem is required then beat well to bruise so that the flavour can be imparted. Stalks keep well in the refrigerator for up to about 2 weeks. When unavailable used grated lemon zest instead or a pared piece of lemon peel. Dried lemon grass is also available as a powder called sereh.

Noodles Many, many different varieties

Oyster Sauce Oriental oyster sauce, a light sauce made from oysters and soy sauce, is frequently used as a flavouring in Thai cooking. It is often used to flavour meat and vegetables during cooking. Despite its name, oyster sauce, it is entirely free from the flavour of oysters, or indeed fish!

Palm Sugar This is a thick, coarse brown sugar that has a slightly caramel taste. is sold in round cakes or in small round, flat containers. It is not strictly necessar and can be replaced with dark soft brow or demerara sugar.

Rice Check your recipe to see whether you require long-grain fragrant Thai rice or 'sticky' glutinous rice before preparation. Most recipes call for the long-grain fragrant variety labelled as Thai but when unavailable then replace with a good-quality basmati or other long-grain rice. When the shorter stickier rice is required then opt for Italian, arborio or medium-round-grain rice. Wash both types very well before use until the water runs clear. This gets rid of any dirt, dust and starch which can ruin the final appearance of the dish.

Rice Vinegar This is vinegar made from rice but with a far less acidic flavour than Western varieties. Cider vinegar makes a good alternative.

Sesame Oil A nutty-flavoured oil, generally used in small quantities at the end of cooking for flavour. Sometimes sesame oil is used with groundnut or sunflower oil for stir-frying.

Shrimp Paste Thai shrimp paste is a dark brown, dry paste made from prawns and salt and is used in small amounts to flavour sauces. Anchovy paste makes a good substitute.

Shrimps, Dried These are strongly-flavoured dried prawns available whole or in powder form. Whole ones should be rinsed before use.

Soy Sauce Choose from light and dark types. The light variety, harder to find, is light in colour but saltier in taste and still full of flavour. It is the best type to use in cooking. The dark variety is darker in colour and often a little thicker than the light type. It is more generally used as a condiment or dipping sauce.

Star Anise A Chinese spice with a distinctive liquorice flavour. It is a spice that is shaped like a star with eight points and is used to flavour meat and poultry dishes in particular.

Tofu Also called beancurd, this is a food made from puréed and pressed soy beans. Sold in flat cakes it has the texture and consistency of soft cheese. Available plain and bland or smoked it is highly nutritious and does take on the flavour of the things it is being cooked with. The type used for stir-frying should be firm so that it does not crumble during cooking and is best cut into cubes for use. Don't be tempted to overmix or stir too vigorously during preparation. A very good ingredient for sweet and savoury dishes – ideal too for vegetarian dishes.

Waterchestnuts Only available in cans but quite acceptable. These give a lovely crunch to a stir-fry, salad or vegetable accompaniment.

Wonton Skins These are thin, yellow discs of dough generally packed in cellophane for easy use. Store in the refrigerator before use and do not allow to dry out or they will become dry and brittle and unsuitable for wrapping around sweet and savoury mixtures that are steamed or fried. Filo pastry makes a good alternative when unavailable.

CREAMED COCONUT

Creamed coconut can be used to make coconut milk. Follow the packet instruction, or, as a general guide, grate 90 g/3 oz creamed coconut into 175 ml/6 fl oz hot water and stir well to blend. The milk made by this method is often very rich and creamy.

NOODLES

Many different varieties of noodles are used in Thai cooking and most can be bought fresh or dried from supermarkets and specialist stores. Most are interchangeable in recipes but the type stated is probably the best to choose. Choose from rice noodles or sticks, medium-flat rice noodles, rice vermicelli or very thin rice noodles, egg noodles and 'cellophane' or very thin transparent noodles. Dried noodles need to be soaked in cold water before using during which time they double their weight. They then require only a very short cooking time. Fresh noodles do not require any pre-cooking and they are cooked in the same way as the pre-soaked dried variety.

INDEX